A Treasury of Toddler Poems

Written by: Howard Eisenberg
Illustrated by: Susan Robinson

Verses to make you laugh when you feel like crying

Digitally Speaking

What was our toddler's first word?

Nope! Neither Mommy nor Dad.

She pointed and proudly proclaimed:

iPad!

Holding Pattern

Why am I pushing this stroller
Holding my toddler? Looking harried?
I had no idea when I bought it
She'd prefer to be carried.

Bedtime Story

When things go bump in the night
It never bothers my head
I know it's only our toddler
Trying to find our bed.

Tactical Decision

Embarrassed by tantrums?
Get this tactic down pat
Stand aloof and exclaim:
"Gosh, whose child is that?"

Floor Walker

Carafes of wine by candlelight
Is how we used to sup
But since our little darling came
We dine mostly standing up.

A Trying Time

Grandma's pumps and Grandpa's oxfords
Big brother's boots. Gosh, what a daughter!
The only shoes that she won't wear
Are the ones that Mommy bought her.

Turncoat

In winter he refuses coats
Could Junior's thermostat be shot?
The only time he'll wear it is
In summer when the weather's hot.

Little Shaver

Liz found her Daddy's shaving cream

And he'd left off the cap

ZAP!

Crisis in the Maternity Ward

Chelsea? Kimberly? Maybe Dakota?
Geneva? Cindy? Not an iota
Of time left to us before it's too late
Gotta name this child and it's gotta be great.

Valerie? Ivy? How about Sasha?
Or would she prefer the sound of Natasha?
We're going nowhere. Our quest's much too aimless
Oops, here comes the nurse. Well...for now she'll be Nameless.

Crib Lib

I'd love to pick up and hug
My adorable little guy
Then again it might be smarter
To let sleeping toddlers lie.

Emily Postscript

Can't find it in Miss Manners' book
But I've a hunch
You should leave a very big tip
When you take a toddler to lunch.

Positively Revolting

Little girls are delicious

Steal your heart by all means

Ain't it a shame

That they turn into teens?

Catastrophe

They won't eat this and won't eat that
The darling little brats
They leave their bowls untouched and then
They crawl right to the cat's.

Art Choke

Someday she'll be a Dali
A Renoir or Van Gogh
At least an Andy Warhol
If not a Picasso.

For the moment though she's stymied
And we admit we're beaten
By our toddler's Artist's Block
She thinks crayons are for eatin'.

Mom in the Middle

It was simply grand at 40
To have my first baby at last
But now faced with reality
I sure hope he'll grow up fast.

Unholy Roller

He will not use the potty
He is stubborn on this issue
But loves going to the bathroom
To unroll the toilet tissue.

Having It All

Their hair's not combed. Breakfast's not eaten
They've broken every rule.
So what? All that I know is ("Sigh!")
They're finally off to school.

Garden Variety

When a praying mantis prays
I wonder if his plea
Is help me out please, Lord
Don't let a kid find me.

Out Of Touch

"Don't touch that!" I command
He's totally unswayed
Looks like I'll have to buy
A toddler hearing aid.

Strategic Retreat

The grandparent advantage
As some of you may know
Is when a tantrum starts
You can just get up and go.

Allergic Reaction

Our kids have lots of allergies
To eggs, to cats, our pup
But their severest allergy
Appears to be to cleaning up.

Shop 'n Stop

I love to shop
I really do
But not with someone
Who is two.

If she's not shouting
"Want those toys!"
She's trailing after
Passing boys.

Regrabbing stuff
I take away
Knocking over
A display.

Peeping into
Someone's sack
Vanishing
Behind a rack.
Throwing fits
And hurling tantrums
Tossing snits
And rave-and-rantrums.

But there's a cure
For all this bother:
Next time I'll leave
Her home with father.

Germ Warfare

He crawls across the kitchen floor
Then calmly licks his hand.
Don't worry. His immunity
Will be just grand.

Gale Warnings

Hurricane? Tornado? Violent spouse?

What wrought this havoc in our house?

You want to know what is it?

Our grandchildren came to visit.

Getting the Brush-Off

Surely there's no greater torture
She screams and struggles to get loose
The brushing of a toddler's hair:
The highest form of Mom Abuse.

Chemistry 101

He's experimenting.

Curb your temper. Just stay loose

When he plops the salt shaker

Into your orange juice.

Body Painting

Our toddler is a nudist
And though I'm not a prude
I'm glad at least she's wearing
Her coat of breakfast food.

Just Looking

Look at the bird! Ooh! Fire truck!

Very pretty tree!

Toddlers open our eyes

To things we've forgotten to see.

Museum Treasures

Our kids adore museums
“Let’s go!” They never fight us.
Alas, they don’t love art
They’ve just got giftshopitis.

Olympic Glow

I envisioned gold medals ahead

Signed her up for swimming school

Paid well in advance but then

She refused to enter the pool.

Cash and Carry

The news for Mom is bad
In the department store:
"Mommy, carry me!
I can't walk anymore."

Fast Food

It's always such
A grand surprise
When toddlers eat
More than their fries.

Wild Kingdom

Why do they make
Such horrid noises?
Simply ‘cause
They’re little boyses.

Careful What You Wish For

We couldn't wait for his first step

But that was ill-advised

Suddenly he's a toddler

And now we're terrorized.

Street Scene

I drag her screaming down the street
In father-daughter duel
People stare. Kidnapper?
Nope. Just late for nursery school.

Calm Before the Storm

My toddler's quite obedient
When I say no more fighting
He stops his punching instantly
Then instantly starts biting.

Flagging Energy

They've barely learned to walk
They cannot pay the tab
But every New York City kid
Knows how to flag a cab.

That's Write

My ballpoint pen is out of ink
But I can make it work, I think
I'll lend it to my toddler small
Who'll make it write upon our wall.

Mealtime Makeover

She's got egg on her face
Oatmeal smeared on her arms
Somehow it just seems
To enhance her charms.

A Shoe-In

Fumbling fingers.

Eager faces.

They're learning to

Tie shoelaces.

Rainy Day Splashathon

They may hate water
In the bath
But puddle-to-puddle's
Their favorite path.

Making the Scene

Why is everybody staring?

What is it they think I've done?

It's not me having the tantrum

It's my son.

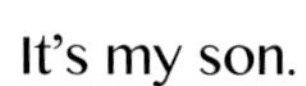

Family Fries

And now a warning to parents:
The surest way to gain weight
Is to have a couple of kids
And eat what they leave on the plate.

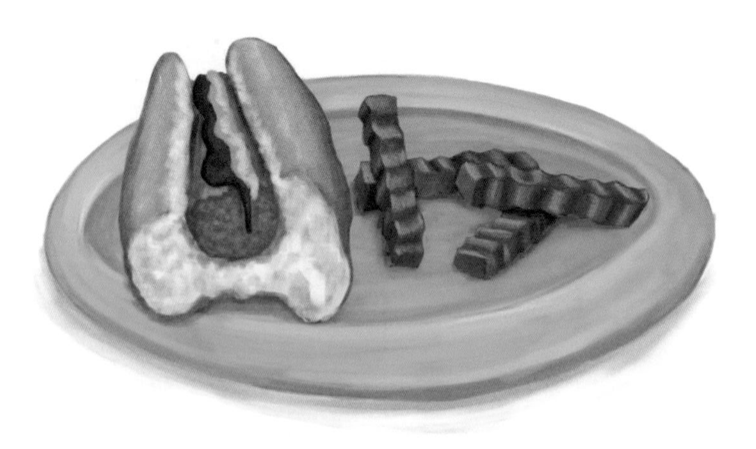